Dear English Major presents

From Graduation to Career Ready in 21 Days: A Guide for English Majors

Alyssa W. Christensen

Acknowledgements

Thank you to Erik Hanberg for inspiration, excellent advice from start to finish, and for helping me navigate the world of online publishing. Big, big thanks to Grace Heerman for contributing an ever-growing list of awesome ideas, revisions, and encouragement.

Many thanks to Omma Christensen, Lauren Selby, McKenzie Lancaster, and Chelsea Phipps for sharing your detail-oriented brains with me! Thank you to editor extraordinaire Tara Jayakar of Raptor Editing for your keen eye.

Thank you to Rebecca King of Renegade Chihuahua for your design expertise and ability to interpret a few adjectives into a beautiful book cover, and thank you very much to Mary Holste for creating a beautiful print version of the book! Thank you to Jacob Christensen, Garrett Collett, Ijeoma Osakwe, and Grace Heerman (again!) for sharing photos of your beautiful, smiling faces!

And finally, thank you to Ben Palmer for excellent career advice, a seemingly neverending supply of patience, and for keeping me (generally) sane.

Thank you!

Alyssa W. Christensen

Table of Contents

Introduction: Congrats! You did it 7

Week 1 9
Day 1: Do your research 10
Day 2: Look the part 12
Day 3: Create a resume 15
Day 4: Collect your writing samples 19
Day 5: Own your online presence 20
Day 6: Create an online portfolio 23
Day 7: Connect with alumni 26

Week 2 28
Day 8: Get organized 29
Day 9: Choose the right jobs to apply for 31
Day 10: Research the jobs you're applying to 34
Day 11: Tailor your resume for Job #1 36
Day 12: Learn how to write a cover letter 40
Day 13: Compile job application #2 44
Day 14: Compile job application #3 45

Week 3 47
Day 15: Hit the "submit" button and officially apply! 48
Day 16: Plan your follow-up strategy 50
Day 17: Prepare for interviews 52
Day 18: Practice answering interview questions 55
Day 19: Review the basics 59
Day 20: Keep learning and bulk up your resume 60
Day 21: Congratulations, new professional! 64

Congratulations, graduate! You did it.

You worked for that English degree, and now it's time to make it work for you.

Let's get down to business.

If you're ready to find your first full-time job, then this book is for you. This guide provides the information and resources you need to successfully navigate the job search process, from finding the right jobs to apply for, all the way to finally accepting a job offer.

In your goal of finding gainful employment, the competition is fierce: there are thousands of other graduates vying for the same positions as you, and you need a way to grab the attention of potential employers. Not only that, but for many, the clock is ticking—your time is precious. We know how hard it is to think about applying for jobs when you've got classes, homework, and internships to take care of, not to mention enjoying the wonderful but bittersweet last days of your senior year! It can be pretty overwhelming. We feel ya. But now that you've graduated, it's time to get down to business.

This guide sets you up for success: follow the instructions we provide each day in order to stay focused, make the most of your time, and land the job you've set your sights on.

You CAN get a job with an English degree.

The first year out of college can be a tough one for any graduate,

Alyssa W. Christensen

not only those with English degrees. But rest assured, English majors: your skills are indeed practical and sought-after by many employers. (We delve into this right on Day 1, so get psyched!) We're not saying that finding these awesome jobs will be easy, and you might not get your dream job on the first try. But there are thousands of employers out there who are searching for candidates with the very skills you honed in college!

There are a few crucial tactics you need to know in order to make a smooth transition from studying Shakespeare and Steinbeck to full-time employment, and this book will guide you every step of the way in 21 days.

Ready?

(Yes. The answer is "YES!") Alright. Let's do this.

Week 1

We're not gonna lie—Week 1 is intense. Do some yoga. Light a candle. Keep calm. Prepare yourself to work hard and kick some serious butt in the job search and application process. By the end of this week, you will have transformed from a brand new college graduate into a viable job candidate with the resume, portfolio, and wardrobe (yep, we go there!) to prove it.

Here's what this week looks like:

Day 1: Do your research.

Day 2: Look the part.

Day 3: Create a resume.

Day 4: Collect your writing samples.

Day 5: Own your online presence.

Day 6: Create an online portfolio.

Day 7: Connect with alumni.

Day 1: Do your research.

Today is about getting your toes wet. Allow yourself the time to explore what kinds of jobs are out there, and narrow down your search.

But wait. What if you don't even know what kind of a career you're interested in? Where do you even start?

Narrowing in on something you're truly passionate about and then actively pursuing it can take years, so don't feel like you need to secure a "perfect" job the first time. Sometimes the best way of figuring out what you DO want to do is by figuring out what you DON'T want to do. Of course, we recommend exploring DearEnglishMajor.com. Dear English Major features dozens and dozens of interviews with English majors with a wide array of careers in different fields.

And yes, they're all using the skills they gained as English majors.

This is just the tip of the iceberg, but a few of those careers include:

Author
Comic Book Editor
Communication Specialist
Community Coordinator
Content Manager
Content Marketing Writer
Content Strategist
Contributing Writer
Copyeditor
Copywriter
Creative Director
Development Editor
Digital Media Manager
Editor
Email Marketing Copywriter
External Relations Manager
Filmmaker
Freelance Copyeditor
Freelance Writer
Grant Writer
Immersive Journalist
Internal Communications Specialist
Internet Marketing Specialist
Journalist
Lawyer
Librarian
Marketing Coordinator
Newspaper Editor
Professor
Proposal Writer
Public Relations Coordinator
Publishing Consultant
Screenwriter
SEO Analyst
Social Media Coordinator
Teacher
Technical Editor
Technical Writer
Video Game Writer

A lot of these titles are vague, and mean different things at different companies. They span a wide variety of industries, and the people featured on DearEnglishMajor.com work at nonprofits, Fortune 500 companies, marketing agencies, publishing houses, newspapers, law firms, banks, schools, universities, software and tech companies, and more. In order to narrow in on a field that interests you, read a few interviews with people in a variety of positions.

We also recommend checking out job search sites like Indeed.com, SimplyHired.com, and LinkedIn.com, for starters (there are many more to explore—don't be limited by this list!). If your college has a job board, then absolutely utilize that as well. Using what your alma mater has to offer is an excellent way to begin connecting with alumni or employers who are specifically interested in your college.

No matter the website you choose to use for your first search, a practical place to get started is to only search for positions in your desired region. Then do a general search for what you're interested in: "writer," "content manager," "social media," "publishing," etc. Click on some jobs you may not have considered before (or even knew existed) and read their descriptions. Some are sure to sound terrible, but some will sound awesome and inspire you to start writing a cover letter. (Don't worry—we go over cover letters in Week 2!)

Save a few of the jobs that interest you, but don't get too attached just yet. Today is about seeing what's out there, and assessing what type of positions are available in your neck of the woods.

Take a deep breath. Your job search journey has officially started!

Day 2: Look the part.

It might seem like putting the cart before the horse, but getting your wardrobe ready for the job search is an important factor in making top-notch first impressions. Sometimes, scoring an interview can take a while, but there may be times when you'll get asked to come in the next day. And when that happens, you'll want to have that collared shirt ironed and your shoes shined.

You also probably have a lot on your mind after Day 1—we said you'd get your toes wet, but some of you probably took a dramatic plunge into the online job pool. Use today to soak in all of that real-world knowledge, and if you don't have anything professional to wear to a job interview (or a first week or two on the job), it's time to go shopping.

You need to market yourself well and looks count. We're not saying that the people who will be interviewing you are shallow, but people are looking for someone who will represent their company well, and part of that is representing yourself well.

Office culture and dress codes these days vary widely—it's not just about tailored suits and pencil skirts anymore. But even if the office of your choice has a reputation for being super casual, you should still show up to your interview dressed for success. You can figure out what's appropriate everyday-attire once you land the job, but for now, you definitely don't want to underdress for an interview. Err on the side of being more dressed up and you'll be safe (but leave the gown and tuxedo for another time).

Anything ranging from "business casual" to "professional" is widely accepted for interview and office attire. The following guidelines are meant to provide you with a place to get started:

Alyssa W. Christensen

These tips will play into your shopping strategy for today:

- Do not wear jeans, leggings as pants, athletic clothing, shorts, t-shirts, tank tops, revealing clothing, sandals, flip-flops, or tennis shoes.
- If you wore it on spring break in Vegas, it's probably not appropriate for your interview.
- Dress modestly; shoulders should be covered, and do not show cleavage or your midriff.
- Do not wear clothes that don't fit correctly. You should be able to sit comfortably.
- Your clothes should be clean and ironed.
- Do not wear strong perfume or cologne.
- Wear makeup and accessories appropriate to the industry.

Day 3: Create a resume.

Today it's time to assess your experience, skills and talents, and how they all translate into a career. While you will revise, edit and tailor your resume to each job you apply for, getting yourself lookin' good on paper is a great (and manageable) place to start.

One of the most challenging things about a resume is that there isn't one set format that everyone follows. However, there are some standard things you'll definitely want to include:

1. Name and contact information
2. Education
3. Experience
4. Skills

Gulp. Feeling overwhelmed?

There's an easy way to break this down!

1. Name and contact information

Start with writing down your name (see, this isn't so bad) and contact information. This should include your email address, phone number, and the city and state you live in. (You can even include your mailing address if you're comfortable with that). If your email address is soccerboi4ever@aol.com or spicychica123@hotmail.com, now is a good time to get a more professional email address before putting it on your resume.

2. Education

Include your college, degree, graduation year, and any other educational courses or programs you have completed. Include any academic honors you have earned. Unless it's specifically asked for by the employer, you don't need to include your GPA, especially if it's below a 3.5.

3. Experience

List out everything you did in college (well — not everything), including extracurriculars, jobs, internships, volunteer roles, and any scholarships and awards you received. (Yes, even if it doesn't feel related to your career goals. You'll be tailoring this later in Week 2, but it will help to get everything out on paper first.) Write down the

Alyssa W. Christensen

years you worked or participated in each item. List out your responsibilities for each item.

Here's an example of what the first draft of this might look like:

Copy Editor of University Science Magazine (2013-2014)
- Edited articles
- Helped writers improve articles

While that's a great place to start, it doesn't really highlight all of the skills that actually go into each task. It's also super vague! What does "edit" mean, exactly? Did it require expert-level knowledge of the AP Stylebook, or the Chicago Manual of Style? Did you edit for punctuation, spelling, grammar, and syntax? Did you fact check?

Your answer is probably "yes!" to all of these! Each of these tasks is an important detail that reveals the expertise and skills that make you qualified for the job. After considering these things, this is what your new and improved responsibilities might look like:

Copy Editor of University Science Magazine (2013-2014)
- Edited all magazine articles for correct spelling, punctuation, grammar and syntax.
- Demonstrated expert knowledge of Chicago Manual of Style.
- Identified specific areas of improvement in articles.
- Worked directly with writers to revise articles.
- Collaborated in team environments.

4. Skills

If you have any additional skills that are not represented in the experience section, then here is your chance to show them off! Are you a PowerPoint whiz? Have a decent knowledge of Photoshop? Include it! Here's an example of what this section might look like:

Skills
- Proficient in PowerPoint.
- Intermediate knowledge of Adobe Photoshop.
- Proficient in HTML5 and CSS.

Objective Statement (Optional): If it seems appropriate, you may choose to include an objective statement on your resume. If you do, we recommend that you include it at the top of your resume. This will help to give recruiters a quick snapshot of what you're all about.

In a clear and concise manner, briefly state what you can offer the employer, and the position you are applying for. Especially since you're new in the world of jobs and most likely applying for something entry-level, it may not be obvious to a recruiter what you're looking for based on your past experience. Keep it at one sentence—you'll go into more detail about yourself later in your cover letter.

Example:
"Seeking a position as a product copywriter in which I will apply my strong writing skills, ability to write under pressure, and my experience as a sales associate."

At this point, don't worry if your resume is a few pages long. In Week 2, we will work on tailoring your resume for specific jobs and condensing it down to one page.

Once you've completed a rough draft of your resume, make sure that you double check these important things:

- Make sure all information is accurate.
- Check for correct spelling, punctuation, and grammar.
- Check for correct contact information.
- Make sure your resume is easy to skim and visually appealing.
- Choose a font that is easy to read.
- Keep job descriptions and responsibilities succinct.

Alyssa W Christensen 17

Need a place to get started? Here's an example of a simple resume template:

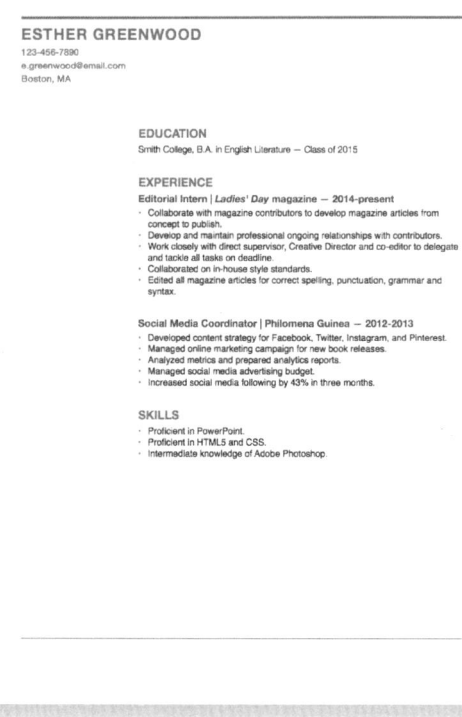

For us writers, being able to pay close attention to detail is an important trait, and sending off a resume with errors of any kind is a big no-no. This includes those basic things like spelling and grammar, but also things like spacing and formatting. Make sure that everything is consistent—your indents are lined up, there aren't any extra spaces, etc. You'd be surprised by how many people make mistakes on these small things, and when competition is fierce, these things matter!

Share your resume with a few English major friends and ask for their edits, and surely, you'll be able to return the favor. No matter how many times you've proofread it, get another set of eyes on it. Now is not the time to cut corners.

Day 4: Prepare your writing samples.

Having a portfolio of your work is a key component of almost every writing-related job application. Most of the time, you will be submitting your portfolio or writing samples online.

You may be tempted to include an awesome eight-page essay you wrote on sea imagery in *Mrs. Dalloway* that earned you an A, but it's not likely to work well in a portfolio. Focus on writing that is for a more general readership, or that is targeted to the audience of the specific position for which you are applying.

1. Start by assessing any writing you have done for extracurriculars during college. Round up everything and make a list of what you have.
2. Select a variety of your best work. If possible, it's good to have several samples to choose from, as you will want to show your most applicable examples to employers if you are only able to submit, for example, two samples of your work.
3. If it's possible to still edit any of your samples (it hasn't been published in a magazine already), then revise them again and have a couple of your English major friends proofread your samples for you. Even though you already completed them, it's not a bad idea to give them another go-over. A potential job is on the line!
4. Organize your samples into PDF files and clearly label each one with your name, "Writing Sample," and title of the content. This will make it easy for you to find in a jiffy when you need to attach something to an e-mail, and it will also make it easier on your potential employer when they're sifting through applicants.

Day 5: Own your online presence.

While you're getting ready to look good in person and on paper, sprucing up your online presence is another key component of your job search. The way you present yourself online is part of your personal brand, and it may be the first place an employer "meets" you. Make a positive first impression!

Clean Up Time

Depending how active you are online, here are a few places you'll want to check and tidy up:

Social Media

You've probably heard about people getting fired for posting something controversial on Facebook, or that employers will look through your photos if they're considering hiring you. Sometimes they do, sometimes they don't, but there's no need to risk it. While you might take measures like making your Facebook profile "friends only," don't rely on this to hide any embarrassing, questionable or unsavory content. If it's online, it's fair game. Who knows—an employee might be Facebook friends with one of your friends, and suddenly everyone can see your personal photos.

Long story short? Take this time to delete anything you wouldn't want the world or your future employer to see and associate with you and your personal brand, no matter how "cool" the company seems. In this day and age deleting sometimes doesn't mean a lot, but it's the best you can do, aside from not posting something negative in the first place. Many of these same rules apply to Twitter, Instagram, and any other social media channels you frequent.

When posting in the future, consider: "Do I want this to be part of my personal brand?" If your boss stumbled upon this photo of you on Facebook (and it totally happens), would you be comfortable with that? That goes for things you say, too. Once you're hired, that probably means no complaining about your boss on social media, either!

Blogs

Is a blog you ranted on every day your freshman year of college still online and public? You might consider taking it down. It probably doesn't represent who you are now as a soon-to-be professional. It's not that you can't be present online, it's just that you should do your best to accurately present who you are today.

Upgrading Your Online Presence

LinkedIn

LinkedIn is an excellent place to connect with other professionals. Fortunately, you are totally prepared to do this since you already created a resume on Day 3. Just plug in your resume and upload a professional headshot!

Speaking of which...

It's time to get an updated headshot photo. Don't have a quality, recent photo of yourself? Then it's time to get one!

If you're serious about your career, then having a professional headshot taken with a high-quality camera is a must. After all, this will be the first impression that many will have of you, and you want it to be a good one. If you don't represent yourself well online, how will you be able to represent someone's company?

If a super high-quality photo is unattainable right now, you still have no excuse for not getting a decent one. Cell phone cameras have come a long way, and it's easy for an amateur to snap a clear, in-focus photo with the latest iPhone that can be used for the small LinkedIn profile photo. Dress up in some of those new professional clothes you bought on Day 2, find some natural light, and have someone snap a photo of you.

Headshot Tips:

- We should be able to see your entire head and some of your shoulders. No crazy close ups on your face—no one wants to see *that* much of you! This also means no full body shots—a LinkedIn photo is small.

- Don't wear sunglasses. You're not James Bond.

- Wear something conservative. You don't need to be wearing a suit and tie, but make sure your shoulders are covered.

- Don't overly edit the photo. A little color boost here and a small touch up there might be okay, but do not add an Instagram-esque filter. It should just be simple, clear, and crisp.

- Make sure the photo is up-to-date. It should look like you NOW, not when you were 30 pounds lighter or had a drastically different haircut. Don't slather on the makeup until you're unrecognizable, either. Be authentic!

- Don't choose a crazy background, and don't choose something that you blend into (if you have jet black hair, avoid a dark black background). The background should be simple and your face should be the focus.

- Consider your expression and what it might say about you. It's about achieving balance: smile to show that you're approachable and easy to talk to, but don't smile so big that it's cheesy or fake. Looking too serious or expressionless is kind of scary and doesn't exactly say "Hire me!"

Does this sound too suffocating? "But I have bright pink hair and a neck tattoo!" No problem! If that's who you are, then that's who you are! The right employer for you will love your lip ring and your mohawk… they just might be a bit harder to find.

Day 6: Create an online portfolio.

Part of upgrading your online presence is creating an online portfolio. If you're pursuing a career as a professional writer, having an online portfolio is an absolute must. It allows you to direct potential employers to a single, permanent space where your work will always be accessible. Even more importantly, it improves your professional online presence and creates a platform on which to market yourself, which is really what finding a job is all about. Not only is this a convenient and easy way to showcase your work, but it shows that you are fairly tech-savvy. It's important to have a strong, unified online presence while on the job search, and for creative professionals, online portfolios are the new business cards.

An online portfolio ensures that your writing samples are accessible at a moment's notice. Plus, they're easily shareable on social media sites like Twitter and Facebook, and you can add your website's URL to your email signature or a business card.

Setting up a website or a portfolio site is pretty easy (and oftentimes free!); it's up to you how complicated or expensive you want it to be.

You have lots of options, and if easy-to-use templates and step-by-step instructions are what you need, then consider creating an online portfolio on websites like Clippings.me, Pressfolios.com, Contently.com, JournoPortfolio.com, Coroflot.com, Behance.net, and the list goes on. Many of these sites will help you set up a basic portfolio in just a couple of hours.

If you want to be able to customize your site more and show off some of your web design skills, then we recommend WordPress.com or Squarespace.com. These options require more legwork, but it's worth it if you're all about choosing your own themes, colors, styles, and layouts. Don't let this intimidate you—the skills you could gain while figuring out how to design your own site are valuable in the workplace! There are tons of online tutorials to get you started.

No matter how you decide to present your portfolio, consult our expert checklist below to ensure your online portfolio is polished, professional and effective.

Things Your Online Portfolio SHOULD Include:

Relevant domain:
Having your own domain name doesn't cost much and it shows that you are serious about being a professional. Use your own name or a business name—it's all about marketing yourself and creating something memorable.

Aesthetically pleasing design:
Treat the design of your website as part of the portfolio itself. You want to show potential employers and clients that you have some web skills, but don't worry—this doesn't mean you have to become a web developer or a coding expert. Many designs are already built for you, and you have the option to customize them if you want. Also keep in mind that what is "hip" in design is constantly changing. You don't want a site that looks like it was built in 2005—things have come a long way since then.

Professional headshot:
Luckily, you're already prepared and have an awesome headshot from Day 5!

Resume:
Whether listed directly on the site or provided as a PDF, including your resume offers an excellent way for potential employers to get a quick picture of your experience. Even a link to your LinkedIn profile is a good option.

Portfolio:

This one is obvious at this point, but if you are going to bother making a website, then it needs to showcase your work! (It's surprising how many professional websites actually lack this.) Include photos of completed projects, samples, screenshots, links, videos—whatever you have. It's best to include a caption with each piece that at least details when it was created and what your contribution was.

Contact info:

A simple email address that you regularly check will suffice. We definitely don't recommend sharing your complete personal address online.

Things Your Online Portfolio SHOULD NOT Include:

Dead pages and faulty links:

Test every link on your page—it doesn't look very professional if you send someone to your portfolio and an important page is broken.

Unfinished design:

Don't send anyone to your site unless it's completely finished! Once you start a page, finish it. (No "under construction" images!)

Out-of-date information:

It's a good idea to give your portfolio a glance every few months. Consider adding a website updating schedule to your calendar as you gain experience and have new writing samples to share.

Spelling or grammatical errors:

The last thing you want is for a potential client or employer to catch an error! Time to call in another favor with one of your English major friends.

Whether you choose to use a simple portfolio option or decide to start a new website from scratch, shoot for a minimum viable product for now. By this, we mean create something that you can point someone to on Day 7. You could easily spend a month perfecting every last detail, but right now, you want to keep your eye on the prize.

Day 7: Connect with alumni.

Today is all about networking. We didn't include "networking" in the title, because to a lot of people, that's a very scary word. Try to simply think of it as connecting with others to form useful relationships. You do it all the time without even realizing it—now, do it with intention and purpose.

Now that you have a resume, a portfolio, and a polished online presence, it's time for you to put yourself out there. One of the biggest benefits of your degree is the alumni network you have access to, yet so many students never take advantage of it!

Career Center

A good place to start is by reaching out to your school's career center. If you've never visited your college's career center, then there is no time like the present! If you don't live nearby anymore, give them a call, or send an email and ask what resources they offer graduates. Explore their website. Share what careers interest you, ask for recommendations, and if possible, have someone look over your resume. See if they can help you reach out to any alumni or other connections in the community. It's what they're there for!

LinkedIn

LinkedIn is an excellent place to connect with alumni; you can filter your search by school, and reach out to those who have found jobs in your field. It's also very likely that your school has an alumni group on LinkedIn that you can join and use to meet other alums. Use the group to ask questions, comment, and interact with others.

Many people remember the struggle they went through to find their first job, or have an experience where someone else helped them out with a referral. They can relate, and will probably be more than happy to help out a fellow alum, whether it's with a piece of advice, an introduction to someone else who can help you, or even a recommendation to an employer in your favor.

Don't forget, this is a conversation. The alumni you reach out to might want to know if a favorite professor is still on campus. Does a certain tradition still happen every year? You can serve as their connection back to their alma mater (assuming they have fond memories of college). Connecting authentically with alumni who graduated even several decades before you is surprisingly easy because of your shared experience. (Also, people generally love talking about themselves!) Be courteous, thank them no matter what they offer, and don't waste their time.

Tip #1: If someone refers you to their employer and you end up getting hired as a result, your connection might be offered a bonus. You could actually help someone make some extra dough, so it may certainly be worth their time to help you if you look like a promising candidate.

Tip #2: Part of dressing for success is having a few business cards up your sleeve! (We mention it now, because we think you should definitely list your new website or online portfolio on your business card.)

Take time today to order some business cards online. At this point, it doesn't have to be anything fancy—you don't even have a job title yet, after all. Order a few (yes, no need to order 1,000). Include your name, phone number, email address, city, and website. We recommend MOO.com and Vistaprint.com.

You did it!

You finished Week 1, and that means you are equipped with the tools you need to tackle Week 2. Onward!

Alyssa W. Christensen **27**

WEEK 2

Roll up your sleeves and make a cup of coffee (or two, or three...). Week 2 is filled with exciting stuff, and this is the week you'll choose your first three jobs to actually apply for. By the end of this week, you'll have resumes, cover letters and writing samples that have all been meticulously and thoughtfully tailored to the jobs at hand. Resist the urge to cut corners, and do your best to give this week 100%—not only are you trying to successfully land your first full-time job, but you're practicing and honing skills that you'll use for the rest of your professional life!

Here's what this week looks like:

Day 8: Get organized.

Day 9: Choose the *right* jobs to apply for.

Day 10: Research the jobs you're applying to.

Day 11: Tailor your resume for Job #1.

Day 12: Learn how to write a cover letter.

Day 13: Compile job application #2.

Day 14: Compile job application #3.

Day 8: Get organized.

Today is about getting things in order and setting yourself up for success. Your head might still be spinning from all the work you put in last week, so take today to regroup and put your organizational skills to work!

1. Set up a spreadsheet that will help you organize your job search.

Here is an example:

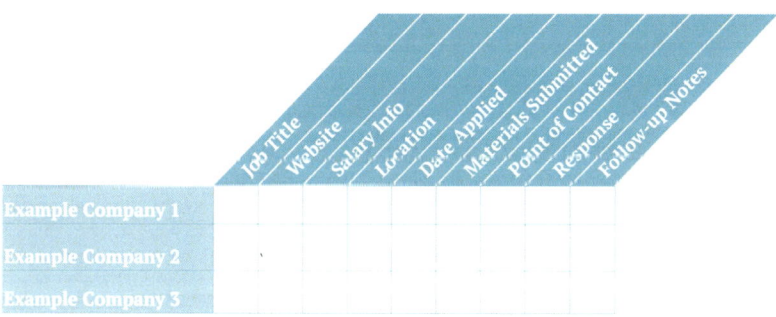

You can download a printable version of this spreadsheet at **DearEnglishMajor.com/downloads**

2. Organize your writing samples.

Did you receive any feedback from your detail-oriented English major pals on your resume or writing samples? Today's the day to make final revisions, save PDF versions of your writing samples, and label them in a way that will make them easy for you to find later. Consider including your name, a brief description or title of the piece, and "Writing Sample" in the title. This might have to be modified once you actually need to submit it, but this is an excellent place to start.

3. Set up a folder on your computer for all of your job application-related documents.

Title the folder "Job Application" and include sub-folders for "Resumes," "Writing Samples," and "Cover Letters." Eventually, you'll want to create folders for each job you apply for, too.

4. If you don't have a calendar or some kind of daily planner, now is the time to get one!

Whether it's a physical planner or a trusty app on your phone, you need to have a calendar that you check regularly. You'll need to write down reminders for when to follow up on applications you've submitted, as well as any interviews you have scheduled. Do not rely on your memory alone for these things. Utilizing a planner is essential in keeping your professional life organized and your stress levels low.

All of this organizing might seem tedious, but it's absolutely worth it (we pinky promise). Not only do you need to be prepared for this coming week of prepping job applications, but if any alumni contact or respond to your inquiries from yesterday, or if a job opportunity suddenly arises, you want to be able to promptly send your resume and any writing samples you're asked for.

Day 9: Choose the *right* jobs to apply for.

Today is about officially zeroing in on the real jobs you want. For the time being, we recommend choosing three that you can focus on and give your all. On Day 1, you took the time to explore job search sites like Indeed.com, SimplyHired.com, LinkedIn.com, and a job board your college may offer. By now you're probably familiar with how to use these sites, and are aware of the types of jobs that are being offered in your city.

The first step is to decide what niche you would like to pursue. Instead of applying for a position as a copywriter, social media manager, *and* a communications coordinator, consider sticking with one type of position for these first three job applications. Choosing, say, just the copywriting positions will simplify the whole process for you (less resume and cover letter revising!), and the copywriting positions will probably vary enough as it is.

This doesn't mean that you need to choose the career you'll have for the next five years right now—you can always change your mind. It's just a place to start, and as writers know all too well: starting is sometimes the hardest part.

Take these things into consideration as you begin your search:

You may find yourself wondering: "Why am I only applying to three jobs? One of my friends had to apply to 20 before they were hired!"
We believe in focusing on quality over quantity, and yes, there is a high chance that you will be applying to more than three jobs... eventually. You might be tempted to fire off your resume in every direction, because something is bound to stick, right? I mean, what if you invest hours into one job application only to be rejected (or worse—never given the time of day)?

We're definitely not asking you to put all of your eggs in one basket, but if you take the time to properly invest in the job applications you have chosen, at the very least you can rest assured that you

Alyssa W. Christensen

truly gave it your best. You have one shot in front of a recruiter, and you want to make it count. Plus, recruiters can usually tell when you've submitted a form resume, half-baked cover letter or blanket inquiry, which reveals that you might not be as interested as the next applicant who obviously spent some time on their cover letter. You're also more likely to make silly mistakes if you don't take your time on each application.

You don't have to meet ALL of the requirements to apply for a job.
Yes, it's counterintuitive: the word "requirement" should be pretty straightforward. But many times—especially for entry-level positions—the requirements in a job listing are purely aspirational and are sometimes not even necessary. Do not let phrases like "minimum of five years experience required" scare you away.

Do your best to reasonably assess your ability to do the job, and your ability to learn what might be necessary to do the job. Do you think you have most of the skills necessary to excel in the position? Have you done something similar in the past?

Watch out for scams.

If you're using a reputable job search site, you're less likely to run into scams. This is more of a problem when you're searching for part-time or freelance work (especially on Craigslist). It doesn't mean that you shouldn't use sites like Craigslist, but it's good to be aware of what you should look for in a legitimate job posting. Just like employers will expect you to include certain key pieces of information in your application, you should expect the same of them.

A job posting that is worth your time will include the following information:

- The name of the employer and a brief description. (Sounds obvious, but if you've ever delved into the "writing gigs" section of Craigslist, you know that even this information can be missing.)
- A position's title and explanation of responsibilities. "Social Media Manager" and "Technical Writer" mean different things at different companies. Being able to see that a company knows what they're looking for is important and shows you that they have

32 *Dear English Major*

their act together.
- A description of the skills and education required. (Keep in mind that oftentimes, "required" = "desired.")
- The type of position and/or duration. Is it full-time, part-time, or contract?
- Some mention of compensation. This could be an exact number, or just whether or not it is salaried or paid hourly. It should also mention if the position offers any benefits (such as health insurance, a retirement plan, or vacation time).

Now, it's time for you to choose those final three jobs. Get excited! One of these could be the beginning of your career.

Day 10: Research the jobs you're applying to.

Today, take the time to learn more about the jobs you've decided to apply for. You're about to invest hours into each application process, and the more you know about each position, the better prepared you'll be to conquer each step.

For each position you've chosen, do the following things:

1. Research the company.

Especially if the company's purpose is not obvious or one you're familiar with, it's important that you have a firm grasp on what they do. Not only will this help you sound intelligent and informed in your cover letter and eventual interview, but it will help you determine if it's actually a company you want to work for! Google the company and find out what the news and employees are saying, and check out their social media presence. Glassdoor.com is another excellent resource with reviews from employees. Yes, this takes time, but if you're going to be potentially giving 40+ hours each week to this company, you want to make sure you know what you're getting yourself into!

2. Research the job position.

Unless you're very comfortable with the job description and familiar with the types of responsibilities involved, take some time to research the type of job you're applying for. See what other professionals out there are saying, learn more about what the responsibilities entail, etc.

3. How do you apply?

Do they just want a resume? Or are they looking for a resume, cover letter, and three writing samples? Are you prepared to apply, or is there additional information you need to put together and supply? Make a list of what's required, and read everything carefully. The last thing you want to do is submit the perfect resume and cover letter... and forget to submit the writing samples they required.

4. Is there anyone in your network you can reach out to?

Check out LinkedIn, and see if any of your connections work at or have worked at the company you're interested in. Do you have any mutual connections? Reach out to connections on Facebook or Twitter—get resourceful! Ask your network what they know about the company, or if there's anyone who could introduce you to someone who works there. It doesn't hurt to ask! Many people are happy to offer their help—they remember what it was like looking for their first job.

Day 11: Tailor your resume for Job #1.

Today it's time to put together your first official resume! Yes, you technically already put together a resume on Day 3, but now it's time to pare it down to a one-page beauty that highlights your best professional self for Job #1. You should **definitely, absolutely** tailor your resume to each job you apply for. Yes, it's time consuming, but it's essential.

Here are some tips to get you started:

Include only relevant experiences.

Let's say you have experience working for your college's newspaper, nannying, and working as a library assistant. If you're applying for a job at a children's book publisher, or as a social media coordinator at a children's clothing company, then including your nannying experience could be a major plus! It shows that you're truly in touch with the subject material and can probably relate more to the customer. However, if you're applying to work as a proposal writer at a law firm, then it's probably best to not include it.

Re-package your roles and responsibilities.

If you're applying for a position as a social media coordinator, then make sure recruiters know about that time you managed your college magazine's Facebook page! Make it front and center by putting it at the top of your list of responsibilities for that position.

Include important keywords.

It's important to keep in mind that some recruiters won't even see your resume if it doesn't contain certain keywords. These keywords are most likely included in the job description, so do your best to include what you can while being honest and authentic. Go through the job posting and make a note of key responsibilities, skills, and qualifications. For example, the employer might require proficiency in WordPress. Your resume might already list "Contributed articles to company blog," but this will go unnoticed when an employer is looking for the keyword "WordPress." If you worked with WordPress, then you increase your chances of being seen by being more specific: "Contributed articles to company blog using WordPress platform." Just be careful—you don't want your resume to become a canned list of keywords you obviously copied and pasted from the job posting.

What if I don't have what they're looking for?

Whatever you do, do not misrepresent your actual skills. No good can come of this.

For example, if your dream job requires proficiency in HTML5, you have three options:

1. If you're proficient, then of course, include this skill in your resume!

2. This might not be the job for you, but you can highlight skills like "quick learner"—they might provide on-the-job training if they find the right candidate. Do not let the fact that a job requires a skill you don't have deter you from the job altogether—lots of employers expect this and are willing to train a new hire if they're the right fit otherwise. But if it seems like it will be a big component of the job, then it's probably not the right fit for you.

3. If you've noticed that several jobs you're interested in require HTML5, consider investing the time in learning it!

It's also worth noting that sometimes, these are just buzzwords used by people who don't know what HTML5 is but assume that the job of the social media manager means they need someone who does. Like we mentioned before, if it seems like a reasonable bet but you're not 100% qualified, we say go for it!

Let's get started.

Begin by opening your resume and the first job you're applying for. Carefully re-read the listing for Job #1, and pay close attention to the job requirements and responsibilities. Which of your experiences best reflects your ability to do Job #1?

For example, if you're applying for a position as a copyeditor, then you'll want to be sure and highlight any copyediting or proofreading experience you have. Once you've selected the experiences you want to include, take a look at the responsibilities and achievements you have listed for each one. Consider moving more applicable bullet points to the top of the list.

Here is what the original from your first resume might look like:

Internship at Publishing Company (2013-2014)
- Managed book submissions.
- Managed all company social media, maintaining the company voice and brand while generating new and compelling content.
- Edited all magazine articles for correct spelling, punctuation, grammar and syntax.
- Identified specific areas of improvement in articles.
- Worked directly with writers to revise articles.
- Collaborated in team environment.
- Contributed articles to company blog.

Considering that you're applying for a copyediting position, you'll want to make it easy for recruiters to see your most applicable skills at a glance:

Internship at Publishing Company (2013-2014)
- Edited all magazine articles for correct spelling, punctuation, grammar and syntax.
- Identified specific areas of improvement in articles.
- Worked directly with writers to revise articles.
- Collaborated in team environment.
- Managed book submissions.
- Managed all company social media, maintaining the company voice and brand while generating new and compelling content.
- Contributed articles to company blog.

What are the other skills, requirements and responsibilities they're looking for? Is it important that you're good with deadlines and able to collaborate on a team? Include experiences that show deadlines are nothing new to you, and that working on a team is something you're well-accustomed to.

Keep in mind that a recruiter might not know much about the job position that's being offered, so you'll want to make it as easy as possible for them to skim your resume and see that you're the right one for the job. Don't make them sift through information that might have them wondering how this qualifies you for the position—make it obvious!

There's a lot to remember with each resume, and we highly recommend using the checklist below to make sure you're staying on top of your game.

Your final resume checklist:
- Make sure all information is accurate.
- Check for correct spelling, punctuation, and grammar.
- Ensure that all contact information is correct.
- Make sure your resume is easy to skim and visually appealing.
- Make sure that all formatting is consistent.
- Choose a font that is distinguished, yet easy to read.
- Keep job descriptions and responsibilities succinct.
- If you have a long list of jobs and achievements, resist the urge to list every little thing you've ever done and focus on the items that are more applicable to the job at hand.
- Limit the length of your resume to one page. (No double-sided resumes, either!)

Resume editing tip:

Instead of reading your resume line by line, consider looking for one particular thing at a time. For example, check that all sentences have periods. Then check that each line is indented at the same spot. Next, check that each title is bolded and formatted the same, and so on. This allows you to focus on one thing at a time.

Re-save each resume that you send. Don't keep modifying one over and over. Having a "master" resume for social media, one for copywriting, and one for editing will be helpful if you apply for a several jobs in a similar field.

Yes, this is time consuming. But it's certainly a waste of time to half-heartedly send off applications that you've put minimal effort into, not to mention the fact that recruiters will be able to tell! **Give it your all, and do it right the first time.** You can sleep easy knowing that you gave it 100%.

Day 12: Learn how to write a cover letter.

Writing a cover letter is much easier if you do so with an actual job in mind, and that's why we've left this task until after you selected your three jobs to apply for. Keep what you learn today handy, since you will write, rewrite and revise a cover letter each time you apply for a new position.

Cover Letter Basics

The purpose of a cover letter is to allow an employer to get to know you beyond what it already says on your resume.

- The entire cover letter should be limited to one page.
- In the heading, include your first and last name, and contact information (mailing address, email address, phone number).
- Include the date followed by the employer's name and address.
- Directly address the person who will be reading your cover letter. Sometimes it is clear who will be reading your letter, and sometimes it's not. Do your best to find out who will be reading your cover letter, and avoid using a blanket "To whom it may concern" whenever possible.
- Close each letter with "Sincerely," and your name.

Here's an example of a cover letter heading:

<pre>
                                          Esther Greenwood
                                           1234 Main Street
                                          Boston, MA 12345
                                              123-456-7890
                                     e.greenwood@email.com

      April 12, 2015

      Jay Cee
      4321 First Street
      New York, NY 10014

      Dear Jay Cee,
</pre>

40 *Dear English Major*

Every cover letter will be (and should be) different, and while you're probably wishing there was a clear-cut formula, this is your chance to be a bit creative and show off your strong writing skills! Start out by aiming for four paragraphs.

Here is a basic cover letter form that you can use as a guide:

Paragraph #1: Introduction

Paragraph #2 and #3: Why are you perfect for this job?

Paragraph #4: Conclude

- State the position you're applying for in the first sentence; make your intentions clear.
- Don't just repeat everything that's in your resume. Use your cover letter as an opportunity to add to what's already on your resume.
- Why are you a good fit for the company? Do you have a personal connection to this company? For example, are you a consumer of the product? You don't need to make anything up if it's not true, but these are the things that can make you stand out amongst other applicants who maybe haven't even bothered to research the company and don't mention it at all.
- What can you bring to the company and the position? What skills, talents, and experiences do you have that can benefit the company? Talk about your strengths and how past experiences equip you for the job at hand.
- Now is a great time to elaborate on other experiences that may play into this role. It may be obvious how an internship at a publishing company will benefit your role as an editorial assistant at a publisher, but it might not be as obvious how your volunteer experience at a seemingly unrelated nonprofit does. Elaborate on this and share how this unique experience makes you an excellent candidate.
- The last paragraph should be fairly short. Use this to make sure your enthusiasm is clear. Succinctly state that you would like to be considered for the position (that is the point of this letter, after all) and wrap it up.

Cover Letter Tips:
- The cover letter is a place where you can demonstrate your strong writing skills. However, avoid using overly verbose language, and

don't abuse the thesaurus. Although a cover letter is a formal piece of writing (so don't say "Hey, my name is..." or "lol"), there's no need to be overly formal. Be authentic.

- Don't focus on your weaknesses or readily address them. "I know that I've just graduated college and don't have much experience, but I think that I have what it takes to succeed in this position." It's not very convincing and it's kind of a downer! (However, this doesn't mean that you need to hide that you're a recent graduate—be proud! Everyone starts somewhere.) Be confident in what you do have to offer, and stay positive.

- Use succinct language to make statements. For example, instead of saying, "I believe that I am a detail-oriented person," just say "I am a detail-oriented person."

- Your cover letter should be easy to read. This includes the actual writing, but also the appearance of it. Choose a standard size 12 font that is easy on the eye, include spaces between paragraphs, and use one-inch borders. Recruiters could be reading hundreds of cover letters each day, and you don't want yours to be especially taxing. Limit your cover letter to one page.

- Don't use a stock cover letter. We know—cover letters are time consuming and exhausting. But if you don't take the time to tailor yours, employers will know... because they've read the same letter a thousand times already from other applicants.

- It's not always possible, but do your best to find out who will be reading the letter, and appropriately address them. (And spell their name correctly!) It shows that you put care into your letter, the same way you'll surely put care and thought into any projects you do for the company once you're hired.

- Don't pack your cover letter with buzzwords and jargon, avoid clichés, and don't parrot back the job description. This comes off as inauthentic, and is just plain boring to read.

- Edit your cover letter! Take some time away from it, and read it out loud to yourself. Send it to a few friends to read, and better yet, send it to folks who have had experience successfully securing jobs. Be open to their feedback.

- This should go without saying, but don't lie. When the competition is fierce, it might be tempting to tell a little white lie here or there. But don't exaggerate your web design skills, and don't oversell yourself. If you do score an interview, you'll only being doing yourself a disservice when it comes time to deliver and you can't. It destroys your credibility and it's a waste of everyone's time.

Word on the street...

At some companies, it's accepted and even expected that you'll do what it takes to stand out. We've heard of people getting creative with their cover letters, whether it's submitting a video in place of the standard one-pager, an over-the-top interactive website, or a tongue-in-cheek reply to a personal ad. All of these things can work, but use your best judgment and proceed with caution!

Now that your resume and cover letter are squared away, is there anything else the application for Job #1 calls for? Do they ask for specific writing samples? Make sure you have everything you need.

Even though you'll probably want to hit that "submit" button right away, resist the urge. Send your resume and cover letter to friends to edit and pat yourself on the back. Your first *real* resume and cover letter are almost ready to go!

Day 13: Compile job application #2.

Today is pretty straightforward—you're going to prepare your application for Job #2. Use the following checklist to stay on task:

Job Application Checklist

Resume
- Re-read job requirements and description.
- Tailor resume.
- Edit resume.

Cover Letter
- Format with correct company and address.
- Write cover letter.
- Edit cover letter.

Writing Samples
- Select appropriate writing samples.
- Retitle if necessary.

Miscellaneous
- Is there anything else that the job application requires?

Day 14: Compile job application #3.

Today you're probably getting the hang of things! It's time to prepare your application for Job #3.

Job Application Checklist

Resume
- Re-read job requirements and description.
- Tailor resume.
- Edit resume.

Cover Letter
- Format with correct company and address.
- Write cover letter.
- Edit cover letter.

Writing Samples
- Select appropriate writing samples.
- Retitle if necessary.

Miscellaneous
- Is there anything else that the job application requires?

Awesome—you finished Week 2!

Week 3 is packed with some exciting stuff, and starts off with a bang: we'll begin the week by finally applying to jobs.

WEEK 3

This week, we begin with officially submitting those three applications you've toiled away on. Take a moment to enjoy and appreciate what you've accomplished, but then it's back to work! You'll be preparing for interviews and learning how to make yourself a more appealing job candidate.

Here's what this week looks like:

Day 15: Hit the "submit" button and officially apply!

Day 16: Plan your follow-up strategy.

Day 17: Prepare for interviews.

Day 18: Practice answering interview questions.

Day 19: Review the basics.

Day 20: Keep learning and bulk up your resume.

Day 21: Congratulations, new professional!

Day 15: Hit the "submit" button and officially apply!

Today, it's finally time to apply to the three jobs for which you've painstakingly prepared resumes, cover letters, and writing samples. What it means to actually "apply" will differ from job to job—for some, you will just be sending your application materials as attachments in an email. For others, there will be forms to fill out online.

No matter what you have to do, read (and re-read) the guidelines for each application to be sure that you follow the instructions you're provided. You don't want to be disqualified from the position just because you made the silly mistake of forgetting to attach writing samples, and it certainly doesn't make for a great first impression.

Use the checklist below to ensure that you've done everything you can to catch any potential mistakes. You can download a printable version at DearEnglishMajor.com/downloads.

Application Submission Checklist

- Re-read application guidelines.
- Ensure you have all components (resume, cover letter, writing samples, etc.).
- Resume
  - Update resume with any edits you received and would like to use.
  - Read resume out loud and look for any remaining errors.
  - Save as PDF (unless otherwise instructed).
  - Label PDF with your name and "Resume."
- Cover Letter
  - Update cover letter with any edits you received and would like to use.
  - Read cover letter out loud and look for any remaining errors.
  - Double check that the company name and address are correct. (When you're juggling multiple cover letters, it's easy to get these confused.)
  - Save as PDF (unless otherwise instructed).

- Label PDF with your name and "Cover Letter."
- Writing Samples
    - Make sure you have the requested number of samples.
    - Save as PDFs (unless otherwise instructed).
    - Label PDFs with your name, "Writing Sample," and brief description or title.
- Miscellaneous
    - Is there anything else that the job application requires?
- Time to submit!
- Update your job search spreadsheet with each job you apply for.
- If anyone referred you to the job, now is the time to let them know that you have submitted your application. If you are sending your application in an email, then mention the referral in the email.

Tip: If you are sending your application via email, here are a few important things to double check:

- Is the email address spelled correctly? (You want your application to actually arrive!)
- Do you have a subject line?
- Are the appropriate documents attached to the email? If it says to include writing samples in the body of an email and NOT as an attachment, then do so.
- Did you proofread your email?

Congratulations! You did it.
You've taken the first big step towards your career.

Day 16: Plan your follow-up strategy.

Now you can kick back, relax, and wait for the responses to roll in. Ha, ha. Just kidding. Today it's time to get right back to work. It's important to have a follow-up strategy for the jobs you just applied for. Too many applicants make the mistake of hitting that "submit" button and thinking there's nothing left they can do. It's also kind of scary—you have no idea what the recruiter is thinking, and you don't want to make the wrong move. It can definitely be tricky!

If you're super lucky, you'll get a quick response. This takes the guesswork out of following up. But more often than not, you won't hear a peep... at least for awhile. The recruiter or employer are busy, as it can be very time consuming to sift through all of the applications they're probably receiving. There are a million reasons why they might not be responding, but just know that in many, many cases, the waiting period is a normal part of the process.

There are a few different things you can do to follow up on a job application you've submitted. No matter the strategy you choose, one thing is certain: you *must* follow up.

Here are some options for how to follow up:

1. Consider bringing your resume, cover letter and writing samples in person in addition to submitting them online. However, you will really need to use your best judgment on this one. If you feel like it's more of a "mom and pop" type operation that requires a personal touch, it might be entirely possible that dropping your application off in person could allow you to meet a key decision maker in the company. If it's a bigger company with more bureaucracy, your efforts might be pointless or even annoying. We advise you to use a personal touch whenever you can, and that means going in person. And yes... wear interview attire when you do!

2. Definitely send a follow-up email. If you were given an email address as a point of contact, then email is your best bet for following up. Wait one week after you submit your application, and if you haven't heard anything back yet, send an email to inquire as to whether or not your application has been successfully received. If no one responds, consider following up again in two to three weeks. If you receive a firm email that says something like "Thank you for following up. We will reach out when we are ready to select a candidate," then it's clear: wait. They're working on it, and you're on their radar.

Also, even if you have a phone number to call, we don't recommend calling to follow up. You might catch someone at a bad time, there's no paper trail, and voicemails can get awkward.

3. No matter what follow up method you choose, remain professional. Be polite in all communication, don't be demanding, and remain patient and friendly, no matter how frustrated you might actually be. Don't reveal any impatience or annoyance if you haven't heard back; the recruiter is probably up to their ears in work. Also, don't turn into a stalker! Yes, sometimes persistence is rewarded. But sometimes it comes off as desperate, stalker-like, and just plain obnoxious. Emailing something like "I'm really disappointed that I haven't heard back yet," "I really need this job," "Are my emails being ignored?" is just a turn off. Don't try to guilt anyone into responding to you or it will definitely backfire.

We know this phase can be very, very frustrating. Especially if you've submitted your application on a website and there is no email address or any other way to contact an actual human. You're left wondering if anyone is even reading the resume and cover letter you spent hours working on, and sometimes it feels like you're just throwing time and energy into a black hole.

It's true: it can take weeks and even months to hear back from the hiring manager, and sometimes you won't hear back at all. Of course, we don't say this to be discouraging, but to let you know you're not alone. This is happening to other people, too, and you simply have to keep trying. Keep your chin up, and start preparing your next round of applications in the meantime.

Day 17: Prepare for interviews.

Today, we're going to cover everything related to interview etiquette, phone interviews, and how to follow up after an interview. (Tomorrow we'll focus on the actual interview content.) Sometimes, the interviewing process can also be a drawn-out ordeal. However, it's possible that you'll get a call from a company that wants to interview with you ASAP... as in, tomorrow. If that does happen, you don't want to be caught off guard.

Here are some basic guidelines that will set you up for success on the big day:

- **Review the company and position.** On Day 10, you researched the company and position, but now it's time to delve into this even more. Spend time exploring the company website, familiarize yourself with their business model, read articles about the company online, and review the job posting.

- **Arrive early.** Have you ever heard the saying "Early is on time, on time is late, and late is unacceptable"? Well, when it comes to being professional, it's definitely true! You don't want to arrive so early that you're a nuisance—10 to 15 minutes is plenty. You'll want a few moments to gather your thoughts and take a few deep breaths. When you're planning your commute to the interview, allow for all kinds of mishaps: horrendous traffic, a flat tire, etc. To be on the safe side, you may even consider arriving a few hours early to work in a cafe that's near the interview location; that way, you'll rest assured knowing that the interview is just a short walk away.

- **Turn off your cell phone.** It definitely won't make a good impression if your cell phone rings and interrupts the interview. And definitely no checking text messages during the interview!

- **Bring hard copies of your application.** Bring a few copies of your resume, cover letter, and writing samples. Oftentimes the interviewer will already have copies of these on hand or can easily pull them up on a laptop, but you will want to be prepared if they don't.

- **Bring a pen and notebook.** If any important information is shared or if you need to schedule a follow-up interview right then and there, you'll want to be completely prepared to take notes. Plus, it shows that you're ready to learn and that you are invested in the opportunity.
- **Make a good first impression.** When you meet someone for the first time, be sure to look them in the eye and shake their hand. Practice your handshake ahead of time! It should be firm (but not crushing)—offering a limp hand is a lackluster way to greet someone.
- **Pay attention to your body language.** Body language speaks volumes, and it can reveal a lot about you. Sit up straight, make eye contact, and smile when appropriate. Avoid engaging in any nervous habits you might have, like biting your nails, or playing with your jewelry, hair, or clothing. And definitely don't chew gum.
- **Remain professional.** No matter how amazing and friendly your interviewer might be, resist the urge to get overly familiar and, for example, add them as a Facebook friend right away. Yes, definitely be warm and friendly, but remain professional. Also, you do not want to come off as desperate. Hinting that you "really need this job" or that "this is my dream job and I really hope you hire me" comes off as overly needy, awkward, and just plain annoying.
- **Mention your referral.** If there is someone within the company who is referring you, be sure to mention it. You want to do your best to ensure that they receive credit for referring you.
- **Follow up.** Absolutely follow up after your interview. As soon as you get home, send an email or card via snail mail to everyone who interviewed you. Thank them for their time and consideration, and mention that you're looking forward to learning more about the opportunity. Keep it short and sweet. This is another chance for you to shine and show that you're invested in this position. Taking the time to say "thank you" will help you stand out from the applicants who do not.
- **If you find out you don't get the job, still follow up.** Don't give up just because you weren't chosen for the position. Be gracious: thank them for their time and consideration, and ask them to keep you in mind for future positions that might be a good fit. This shows that you're still interested, and who knows? You might have been their #2 choice, and it might have been a hard decision. If the first

candidate doesn't work out or another position opens up, hopefully you'll be top of mind!

What if they ask for a phone interview?

Phone interviews can be tricky—since you can't see the person, you don't have as many cues to inform you of how best to respond. But phone interviews are a common part of the interviewing process, and we recommend approaching them the same way you would an in-person interview.

Here are a few tips:

- Make sure your phone is fully charged.
- Make sure you are in a quiet space with excellent reception.
- If you live with others, let them know that you have a phone interview and should not be disturbed.
- Have your resume, cover letter, writing samples, and any additional notes in front of you.
- Have a pen and notebook at the ready for taking notes.
- Pay attention to your body language, as this can affect the way you speak and influence the frame of mind you're in. Sit up straight or stand up, and don't lounge on the couch or sit in bed.
- Speak clearly so the interviewer doesn't have to struggle to hear you.
- Prepare a list of questions for the interviewer beforehand (see Day 18).

Day 18: Practice answering interview questions.

One of the biggest mistakes people make before they head to an interview is that they don't practice answering potential interview questions. They think that just reading over their resume and cover letter is adequate preparation, or that reading a few interview question examples should do the trick. But practicing answering questions is essential in being as prepared as possible.

We recommend writing down your answers as you think them through, and then practicing them out loud. You shouldn't be memorizing anything word for word, but rather getting comfortable with talking about certain topics and specific experiences. This will help you communicate your ideas clearly in the interview—you will have already thought through them carefully, and when you're nervous, you'll be thankful that you took the time to get your thoughts in order!

There are hundreds of questions you could be asked, and there's no realistic way to prepare for *everything*. But by choosing a few questions to focus on, you will set yourself up with a solid framework to build on when you're in the actual interview. So even if you're not asked the specific question you prepared, that information will probably come in handy when answering another question.

We're going to address a few common questions to get you started in the right direction. You'll also find plenty of examples of potential interview questions in this section as well. Good luck!

Tell me about yourself.

This popular interview "question" isn't actually a question. Suddenly, all of those answers you prepared aren't so useful. You're speechless! Where do you start?!

Have you ever heard of an "elevator speech"? The idea behind the elevator speech is that if you ran into someone important in an elevator and had until the elevator reached their floor to sell them on something, you should be able to do so in 30 seconds or less. Of course, in order to do this, you need to have a clear idea of what you're selling.

Alyssa W. Christensen

The same is true for your answer to "Tell me about yourself." This is your opportunity to show them your true self, beyond your resume and experiences. Practice what you want to tell the interviewer about yourself in 30 seconds or less. While you should address your career aspirations, this is also an opportunity for you to be a real person with family, friends, hobbies and passions. However, avoid telling your life story and sharing anything overly personal. It's a fine balance of being both personable and professional. Be genuine and keep things positive!

Why do you want this job?

This answer might be so obvious to you that you don't even know how to put it into words. "Uh... because I want to work here? Because I need to make money? Because I... have an English degree? I want this job because... I love writing?"

Okay, that's a good start. But it's kind of boring. Instead, try providing more examples and show why you want the job. For example, if you're applying to be a contributing writer at a food magazine, you could start by saying, "I want this job because I love writing, especially about food. One of my favorite things is trying out new restaurants and exploring the cuisine of different cities, and cooking with my family is an important part of my life. So combining both worlds feels natural and is an exciting prospect for me."

There we go. It shows you're genuinely interested in the subject matter, and you sound like a nice person to work with. Check, check.

Why should we hire you?

It's time for your elevator speech! With this one, you need to be confident, but not cocky. Consider what you have to offer that makes you unique. Sure, you are a great writer and responsible—but so is everyone else. What sets you apart from the crowd? What strengths can you bring to the company?

What are your weaknesses?

This question is just plain evil! You don't want to say anything to make yourself look bad, but you also need to be honest. (And yes, you do have a weakness, so if you can't think of anything, think harder.)

When you share your weakness, consider sharing the way you deal with it or are trying to improve. For example: "If I have a lot to do, I can get pretty stressed out. But in college I found that it really helped if I kept a detailed calendar and a daily to-do list. I would still get stressed, but I could at least rest assured knowing that I had a plan in place." See? You have weaknesses, but you have found ways to manage them.

More examples of interview questions:
- What are your strengths?
- Where would you like your career to be in five years?
- How would your friends describe you?
- What accomplishment are you most proud of?
- What kind of environment do you work best in?
- How do you handle pressure?
- What do you know/like about our company?
- What could our company do better or differently?

Many questions interviewers ask are behavioral questions. This means that you're asked to demonstrate something about yourself through a story or by answering a "what if" scenario.

Here are a few examples to consider:
- Tell me about a time you led a project.
- Tell me about a time you went above and beyond expectations.
- Tell me about a time your work was criticized. How did you handle it?
- Tell me about a time you made a mistake.
- Give an example of a time you had a conflict with a coworker. How did you handle the situation?

Especially when you're under pressure, it can be hard to think clearly. Luckily, there's a simple method called the STAR Method that you can use to organize your thoughts as your tell your story. Here it is:

1. SITUATION: What was the situation?

2. TASK: What was your task or goal?

3. ACTION: What actions did you take to get there?

4. RESULTS: What were the results?

And of course, be prepared when the interviewer asks if YOU have any questions for THEM. You should definitely ask a few thoughtful questions, so come prepared. A few questions that can show you're really dedicated to the role include the following: "How do you hope your company will grow in the next year, and how could I contribute to that growth?" and "What are some of the most important qualities you hope someone in this position will have?" If you don't have any questions left about the position, ask the interviewer what they like about working at the company, or another question about their job.

Tips:

- **Don't be afraid to stop and think.** When you're asked a question, you might be tempted to blurt out the first thing that comes into your head just so you don't have to endure an awkward silence. If you don't have the perfect answer on the tip of your tongue, take a moment to think and give consideration to the question. Saying, "That's an interesting question..." or "Let me give that some thought..." are good ways to let the interviewer know you're thinking about it.

- **Don't ramble on just to fill the silence.** Yes, you definitely need to give more than one-word answers. But don't just try and fill the silence, and don't go on and on about any one topic. Get to the point, and wrap it up.

When the interview is over, ask about the next step. When and how should you expect to hear from them? What is a good way to follow up? And finally, thank them for their time and consideration.

Day 19: Review the basics.

Today is about heading back to elementary and junior high school: it's time to review the basics. Yes, we're serious. Your college classes probably didn't cover much in terms of grammar and punctuation—you were supposed to have already mastered it all before you got there, right? But it's likely that a few of those rules have slipped between the cracks, and you may have forgotten (of course, only momentarily...) when to hyphenate something, or where to stick that apostrophe. No judging here. There are a lot of rules to keep track of!

Some employers might require you to take an editing test (especially if it's an editing position), or write something on the spot. And of course, once you land the job and everyone finds out you're a grammar guru, you'll be their go-to grammarian when they can't figure out whether it's "affect" or "effect."

If you already know that the position you applied for calls for knowledge of the AP Stylebook, then buy it if you don't own it already and start studying up!

Day 20: Keep learning and bulk up your resume.

Today, assess what you can do to improve your current skillset. What skills were listed in the job positions you applied for, and do you have all of them yet? What skills did you find in jobs that you want one day, but definitely aren't qualified for (yet)?

While you're in the limbo stage, take time to work on improving yourself and your resume. From learning the ins and outs of Photoshop to working on new writing samples, we have several ideas for how you can make yourself a more attractive job candidate now and in the future.

Learn a new skill that complements your writing skills.

These days, writing well and having excellent editing skills alone just don't cut it! Employers will expect you to have a few other handy talents up your sleeve. Focus on learning things that complement the writing skills that you already have. For example, are you familiar with WordPress? Do you have a working knowledge of Adobe Photoshop or Illustrator? Can you easily switch between a Mac and a PC? Can you effectively implement SEO strategies into your writing? Can you create an email campaign from scratch? Many of these things are naturally integrated with writing and will help to transform you into a more dynamic job candidate.

Of course, you don't have to become an expert on everything. Start by reading over the requirements of the jobs you applied for, and other positions that appealed to you. What skills are mentioned most often?

Use free online resources. There are tons of online tutorials and entire websites dedicated to showing people how to do all of these things and more. Use the glorious internet to your advantage, or head to the library. Be resourceful!

Explore different types of writing.

Having an English degree does not automatically qualify you to write anything and everything. For example, depending on the company, a copywriting position might require a very specific type of writing. Maybe you'll be expected to translate the thoughts of a business owner into copy for the homepage of their business website in the "voice" of the brand. Maybe you'll be asked to write short, punchy copy for a series of billboard advertisements.

If your potential job opportunities ask for experience in a certain type of writing, take time to scour the web for examples, tips, and how-tos. There's an endless supply of educational resources online these days, including classes, video tutorials, ebooks, and websites. The best part? Many of them are even free!

Work on more writing samples.

It's finally time to write for fun! (Unless you consider writing cover letters fun. If so, more power to ya.) Now is the perfect time to work on a personal essay to submit to your favorite website, or see if you can become a contributing writer on a blog. Of course, it's important to pursue your passion for writing for your own personal satisfaction, but it's also a great way to bulk up your portfolio and provide writing samples to potential employers.

As a writer, it can be a huge asset to get your name in "print." Check out some of your favorite blogs and media outlets, and see if they take article submissions. Many mid-sized online publications receive a lot of their content from contributors—you don't have anything to lose by sending an inquiry email to see what opportunities may be available.

You might also consider starting your own blog. If you set up a website or online portfolio on WordPress or Squarespace, adding a blogging component is easy. We also recommend Medium, another excellent platform for bloggers. Having your own blog is a great way for you to have control over what you put out there and generate more writing samples.

Network.

There it is again... that scary word. Many people read about networking and put their foot down. "Nope. If I have to network to find a job, then I guess I won't be finding a job!" It's time to get over this fear, and get over it fast. And you know what? We have a feeling that a few of the ideas we're about to suggest will actually sound enjoyable to you. Here are a few suggestions for ways to network:

- **Connect with writers in your area.** Meetup.com is a great resource for connecting with folks who live in your city who also have similar interests as you. See if you can join a writing-related group and make a few new friends. This is an excellent opportunity for you to have some camaraderie in the job search, solicit feedback on your work, and develop a community that looks out for each other.

- **Connect with other professionals.** It's time to really think outside the box. Consider all of the people who might need a writer: business owners, graphic designers, web developers, marketing firms, etc. The list is a seriously long, long, long one. Don't miss the opportunity to meet new people who might have a need or know about a job opening. You might think that you have nothing in common with that graphic designer you met at a friend's birthday party, but who knows—they could be working on a project that needs a writer!

- **Join professional organizations in your field of interest.** Becoming a member of a professional organization helps expose you to the social scene and opportunities in your desired field. Many professional societies offer valuable resources to job seekers, and some even have job listings right on their websites. Here are a few organizations that might interest you: Society of Professional Journalists, American Copy Editors Society, Society for Technical Communication, American Marketing Association, Social Media Professional Association, Grant Professionals Association.

- **Go to networking events.** Whether it's through your alma mater or a professional organization you've joined, go to networking events whenever you can! When you do attend these events, we know that sometimes it can be hard to figure out what to do. We recommend setting a simple goal, something like "Meet three new people." Shake hands, give them a business card if you have it, and just have three good conversations. Ask about a person's hobbies and interests, and share yours. If they ask what you do, tell them you're looking for a job in your field, but keep in mind that there's no need to grease the wheels or try to land a job on the spot. People want to work with people they like. So go, meet three new people, and then call it good if you're not really enjoying yourself. You hit your goal and became a little more practiced in marketing yourself.

Day 21: Congratulations, new professional!

Okay, so today might not be the exact day you get hired. In fact, it might take awhile. There are so many things that are out of your control in the job search process, and it can get pretty frustrating when it feels like you're putting in tons of work and not getting anywhere. Do your best to focus on what you *do* have control of—the different components of your application, how much you prepare for an interview, how you follow up, and the effort you put into networking.

Money Talk

At some point in your interviewing process, salary will come up. It might not happen in the first interview, but it will eventually! Sometimes, there will have been a salary or hourly rate listed along with the job posting. If you're asked "What are your salary expectations?" you'll want to be ready with an answer.

Avoid answering with an exact number at first, and instead, consider saying, "I would really need to consider the entire compensation package you're offering before discussing any specific numbers." Benefits can be worth a lot, and you'll need to take this into consideration.

When you haven't had a full-time job before, it can be hard to know what's reasonable. Especially if the job posting did not list a salary estimate. When it is time to ask for a specific salary, there are a few things you can do to prepare for what that number should be. Do some research beforehand; Glassdoor.com is a good place to start. What are similar positions in the industry offering in terms of salary? What are other similar job postings offering? Come up with a number to ask for in case you're asked. You definitely don't want to say, "I'm not sure," "I don't know," or "Whatever is fair."

The Offer

When you are offered the job, it will come with an official job offer, usually a PDF document listing your pay rate, vacation time, job title, and benefits. You might be tempted to say "yes" as fast as you can. Take a moment to consider why you're worth more. What added value do you provide the company with over other applicants?

It can be daunting, but always ask for at least a little more. Do your best to push past any fears you may have about asking for more money, and don't chicken out. They will not be insulted; it's expected that you will ask for more money, and they may have even lowballed your offer so they have room to move up.

Let's say they offer you the job at $35,000/year. You can say, "That's wonderful! Thank you, and I'm very interested in this position and all the company offers. From the research I've done, I believe that my skills can bring real value to your company above $35,000. I would like to ask for $38,000."

There are three things that can happen when you ask for more money:

- "No, $35,000 is our final offer." Then you are left to decide if you want to accept it or not. You can always ask for a raise later.
- "We can't do $38,000 but we could go up to $36,500."
- "Okay, we can do $38,000."

If they are unwilling to meet your price, consider asking for another week of vacation or some other benefit. You can also ask for a salary review in six months based on your contribution to the company.

Another important reason to ask for more money: it can be hard to make up the difference through raises or promotions. These are things that will most likely be based off of how much you're already making.

What's next?

Once you are hired, the real, real work is just getting started. Take a moment to celebrate, but don't rest on your laurels. Once you start a job, you should already be thinking about your next job.

Wait, what?

That might sound kind of crazy, and we don't mean that you should only stay a few months then jump ship. (In fact, you should try to stay at your first full-time job for at least a year.) What we mean is that it's important to be strategic. At work, take on challenges, say "yes" to new opportunities that arise, learn as much as possible, and make new friends. These are all chances for you to stand out, work towards getting promoted or secure some awesome references for the next job you apply for.

Do you have a dream job in mind? Did you find something amazing in your job search only to realize that you weren't anywhere close to having the experience necessary? Use this knowledge to inspire and inform your decisions.

Dear English Major,

Congratulations! You are well on your way to having a fulfilling, successful career!

The last 21 days have been filled with hard work, and in that time you've gained valuable skills that you will use for the rest of your life.

Of course, there's always more to learn, and we're here to help! Visit DearEnglishMajor.com to explore our extensive and ever-expanding interview archive. There, you can find invaluable job search tips from professionals who have been in your shoes. You can also visit DearEnglishMajor.com/forum to connect with other English majors, job seekers, and professionals in your field. Ask questions, swap stories, and meet other recent grads who are going through the same thing you are!

You worked super hard for four solid years to complete your English degree, and you deserve the chance to show off those hard-earned skills at a job you love. You have what it takes. Now go get 'em.

We wish you the very best in your job search!

Alyssa W. Christensen

About the Author

My name is Alyssa W. Christensen and I'm the creator and English major behind DearEnglishMajor.com. After graduating from college, I had no idea what kind of career I wanted to pursue. (Not only did I attend a liberal arts school, but my emphasis was in creative writing, specifically poetry, which didn't exactly set me up on a lucrative career track.) My idea of what I could do with an English major was limited, and even after an internship at a publishing company, I still felt like my options were few and far between. But after some serious searching, countless cover letters, my first couple of jobs and diving into the world of freelancing, I learned that there are a ton of options out there for us wordsmiths!

My goal is for DearEnglishMajor.com to be a place for current or recently graduated English students to gain knowledge and a sense of direction regarding their careers. A big part of this includes featuring stories from people who are pursuing careers that have resulted from their English degree, no matter the shape or form.

—Alyssa